THE OFFICIAL
HEART OF MIDLOTHIAN
ANNUAL 2019

Written by Sven Houston
Designed by Lucy Boyd

A Grange Publication

© 2018. Published by Grange Communications Ltd., Edinburgh, under licence from Heart of Midlothian. Printed in the EU.

Photographs © SNS Group

ISBN 978-1-912595-09-9

CONTENTS

CAPTAIN'S WELCOME

FIVE OF THE BEST: SEASON REVIEW

DID YOU KNOW? STEVEN NAISMITH

SPOT THE BALL

WORDSEARCH

YOU ARE THE REF

DID YOU KNOW? HARRY COCHRANE

PLAYER PROFILES

THAT TIME WE PLAYED

WHERE'S JOCK?

DID YOU KNOW? OLLY LEE

TEAM PHOTO

PLAYER OF THE YEAR AWARDS

BIG TYNIE QUIZ

'98 DINNER

DID YOU KNOW? UCHE IKPEAZU

MY TOWN

QUIZ ANSWERS

WELCOME

HELLO AND WELCOME TO THE OFFICIAL HEART OF MIDLOTHIAN FOOTBALL CLUB ANNUAL 2019.

Within the pages of this year's annual, you can read all about the 2017/18 season and get to know more about me and my teammates.

Last season was a tough one for the club as we didn't quite reach the standards that we expect of ourselves. That being said, there were some great highlights, such as the 4-0 win against Celtic and, of course, the Derby wins against Hibs. Another big plus was the opening of the magnificent new Main Stand at Tynecastle Park.

I am sure all Hearts fans will agree that the most important thing for the club was to stay put at our home in Gorgie. We now have a stunning stadium that can host 20,000 supporters and I believe the club has a very bright future in store.

In the summer of 2018 we brought in a host of new faces in order to improve the team ahead of the 2018/19 season. A club like Hearts should always be fighting it out near the top of the table and in the domestic cup competitions. I can assure you we will all be doing our utmost to bring more special moments to our supporters.

I continue to draw immense satisfaction from being the captain of our fantastic club. Running out in front of the Hearts supporters with the armband on gives me an enormous sense of pride and I would like to thank every one of you for your continued support.

Hearts, Hearts, Glorious Hearts!

Christophe Berra
Captain

FIVE OF THE BEST

2017/18 proved to be another eventful season for the boys in maroon. The construction of the new Main Stand at Tynecastle meant the Jambos didn't return to their Gorgie home until November, by which point they had played no less than seven away fixtures. BT Murrayfield was used as a temporary home, however, there's no place quite like Tynie. Over the next few pages, we take a look back at the five most memorable Hearts victories from the 2017/18 season, starting with THAT win over the Invincibles...

Hearts 4-0 Celtic
17th December 2017
Tynecastle Park

16-YEAR-OLD HARRY COCHRANE!

The teenager grabbed his first senior goal in spectacular fashion, rifling in a low shot to put Hearts 1-0 up against Celtic. From then on in, it was one big party at Tynecastle...

MAKING HIS MARK

Harry Cochrane and Kyle Lafferty celebrate the Jambos' opening goal.

NOTHING TO SEE HERE

Don Cowie can't resist giving the Celtic skipper a wee tap on the head!

DREAMLAND

The Captain joins Kyle Lafferty and the rest of the boys to celebrate David Milinković's strike as Hearts go 3-0 up against the Champions.

SPOT ON!

Milinković fires home Hearts' fourth and final goal of the afternoon as the Tynecastle crowd erupts!

LET'S ALL DO THE POZNAN!

It was party time in Gorgie as Christmas came early! The Wheatfield Stand responded with this spectacular celebration midway through the second half.

Hearts 1-0 Hibs
21st January 2018
Tynecastle Park

LET BATTLE COMMENCE

The teams emerge for the Scottish Cup Edinburgh Derby at Tynecastle!

BETTER LATE THAN NEVER

With just minutes remaining, the tie looked certain to head to a replay with neither side able to grab a winner. Until, that is, a corner from the right was headed down by Christophe Berra, enabling Don Cowie to scramble the ball over the line to spark scenes of jubilant celebration in Gorgie!

GET IN!

The Skipper is swamped by ecstatic teammates as the Jambos' late winner sealed another Derby Day victory for the Jam Tarts.

JUMPING FOR JOY

The Hearts bench reacts to the sound of the full-time whistle!

EDINBURGH IS MAROON

Captain Christophe celebrates at the full-time whistle.

JOB DONE

Manager Craig Levein congratulates the Skipper at full-time.

11

Hearts 3-0 St Johnstone
10th February 2018
Tynecastle Park

FIRST LAFF

All smiles from Kyle Lafferty after putting Hearts 1-0 up against St Johnstone in the Scottish Cup 5th Round tie.

GOAL OF THE SEASON

Demetri Mitchell connects with the ball and within seconds, he's scored what Hearts fans would go on to vote as the goal of the season!

BACK OF THE NET!

No chance for the Saints goalkeeper as Demetri's strike flies into the top right corner.

HAPPY DAYS

Kyle was the first player to congratulate Demetri on his stunning goal that put Hearts 2-0 up.

THUMBS UP

The Gaffer gives his seal of approval on an impressive performance by the Jam Tarts.

TASTES LIKE VICTORY

Kyle wheels away in celebration after effectively putting the game to bed with his second, and Hearts' third, goal of the afternoon.

Hearts 2-0 Aberdeen
7th April 2018
Tynecastle Park

UP AND RUNNING

Kyle Lafferty and Naismith celebrate the Jambos' opening goal.

NAISY DOES IT

Steven Naismith puts Hearts 1-0 up against the Dons!

TWO IN TWO!

Just two minutes after Naismith's opener, David Milinković broke into the box and doubled Hearts' advantage!

DO THE MILINKOVIĆ!

David gives the fans what they want: his trademark celebration!

STRONG AS THE OLD CASTLE ROCK

John Souttar was in fine form at the heart of the maroon defence as the Jambos kept the Dons at bay for 90 minutes.

RESULT!

Steven Naismith was a happy man after seeing off Aberdeen.

2-0 Hibs
May 2018
astle Park

THE OPENER!

e Lafferty embraces Hearts'
an after breaking the deadlock
he final Derby of the season.

THAT FEELING

Joy for Lafferty after putting Hearts
1-0 up against the Hibees.

FOR THE BADGE

Lafferty runs to the crowd
after his goal.

BACK IN FRONT

Hibs equalised but Steven Naismith restored Hearts' advantage with a powerful header!

JOB DONE!

The Jambos applauded the fans after sealing another Derby victory.

TURF'S UP!

Within minutes of the full time whistle, tractors took to the Tynie turf to start digging up the pitch in preparation for a new hybrid surface being installed over the course of the summer.

DID YOU KNOW?
STEVEN NAISMITH

BORN: 14TH SEPTEMBER 1986
PLACE OF BIRTH: IRVINE, SCOTLAND

Stevie made his professional debut for Kilmarnock on April 24th 2004 when he came on as a substitute against Hibs.

His first goal in senior football was against Hearts! It came in a 2-2 draw between Hearts and Kilmarnock in February 2005.

In August 2007, Stevie signed for Rangers for a reported fee of £1.9 million.

In November 2007, he made his Champions League debut as a substitute against FC Barcelona at the Nou Camp.

Stevie won three league titles with Rangers, as well as one Scottish Cup and two League Cups.

He scored a total of 33 goals in 132 games for the Ibrox club.

In July 2012, he joined English Premiership side Everton.

Stevie scored 26 goals in 123 appearances for the Toffees before moving to Norwich City.

In January 2018, he returned to Scotland on a loan deal with Hearts.

Stevie re-joined the Jambos in the summer of 2018 and will remain on loan until the end of the season.

SPOT THE BALL

CAN YOU SPOT WHICH IS THE REAL BALL IN THE PHOTOS BELOW?

ANSWERS ON PAGE 60-61

WORD**SEARCH**

FIND THE HEARTS RELATED WORDS IN THE GRID.
WORDS CAN GO HORIZONTALLY, VERTICALLY AND
DIAGONALLY IN ALL EIGHT DIRECTIONS.

G	C	T	L	R	D	J	R	B	F
B	H	O	A	R	R	E	B	B	N
N	N	L	C	D	V	C	K	S	I
E	A	E	L	H	K	Q	O	G	K
I	E	V	L	A	R	B	N	D	P
G	L	E	R	N	M	A	R	V	E
R	C	I	W	A	L	A	N	B	A
O	A	N	J	E	R	P	L	E	Z
G	M	M	E	G	X	L	K	Z	U
S	O	U	T	T	A	R	J	M	F

BERRA   **JAMBOS**   **SOUTTAR**
COCHRANE   **LEE**   **ZLAMAL**
GORGIE   **LEVEIN**
IKPEAZU   **MACLEAN**

ANSWERS
ON PAGE
60-61

YOU ARE THE REF

EXTRA BALL IT IS THE LAST MINUTE OF INJURY TIME AT THE END OF A MATCH, THE BALL IS IN THE CROWD AND THEY REFUSE TO HAND IT BACK FOR THE THROW IN TO THE OPPOSITION. THE TAKER GRABS THE SPARE BALL FROM THE BALL BOY, TAKES THE THROW IN AND, JUST AS HIS TEAM MATE HEADS IT IN, THE ORIGINAL BALL IS THROWN BACK INTO THE AREA. WHAT DO YOU DO?

SUPER SAVE A GOALKEEPER SEEMS TO MAKE A WORLD CLASS FINGERTIP SAVE AND IS CONGRATULATED BY HIS DEFENDERS – HE EVEN PUMPS THE AIR – BUT AS THE OPPOSITION TRY TO TAKE A QUICK CORNER YOU ARE CONVINCED THAT THE KEEPER NEVER ACTUALLY TOUCHED THE BALL, YOUR LINESMAN ISN'T SURE SO WHAT DO YOU DECIDE?

ONE-ON-ONE A STRIKER IS THROUGH ON GOAL IN A ONE-ON-ONE WITH THE OPPOSING GOALKEEPER. HE IS PULLED DOWN BUT AS YOU BLOW YOUR WHISTLE AND SIGNAL FOR A PENALTY, YOU SEE THE BALL ROLL ON INTO THE NET. WHAT ACTIONS DO YOU NOW TAKE?

EMBARRASSING MOMENT THE SCORE STANDS AT 2-2 IN THE DYING SECONDS OF A MATCH AND, AS A SHOT COMES FLYING TOWARDS YOUR FACE, WELL OFF-TARGET OF THE GOAL, YOU INSTINCTIVELY PUT YOUR HANDS UP TO SHIELD YOURSELF. YOU ARE THEN HORRIFIED AS THE BALL FLIES INTO THE NET. WHAT NOW?

RUGBY TACKLE A LONG BALL FORWARD TOTALLY BAMBOOZLES THE OPPOSING GOALKEEPER AND THE BALL BOUNCES OVER HIS HEAD AS HE RUSHES OUT TO INTERCEPT IT. A DEFENDER AND TWO ATTACKERS CHASE AFTER IT AND THE DEFENDER RUGBY TACKLES THE STRIKER IN FRONT TO THE GROUND. THE OTHER ATTACKER IS CLEAR THOUGH AND TAPS THE BALL INTO THE NET. WHAT IS YOUR DECISION?

PENALTY SHOOTOUT IT'S A CUP GAME AND YOU ARE INTO EXTRA TIME. THE HOME TEAM'S STAR STRIKER GETS INJURED AND CAN'T CONTINUE. ALL THE SUBSTITUTES HAVE BEEN USED SO THE HOME SIDE HAS TO PLAY ON WITH ONLY TEN MEN. THEY MAKE IT TO THE PENALTY SHOOTOUT AND THE SAME STAR STRIKER WANTS TO TAKE A PENALTY AS HE NOW SAYS HE IS FIT AGAIN AS THE INJURY HAS PASSED. DO YOU LET HIM?

ANSWERS

EXTRA BALL If the original ball that is thrown back into the penalty box hasn't interfered with play in your opinion then you award the goal! If, however, the ball has interfered with play, you must disallow the goal. You need to be sure!

SUPER SAVE It is your decision, decide quickly and stick to it regardless of what the players and crowd think. If you think the goalkeeper didn't touch it then award the goal kick and not the corner.

ONE-ON-ONE Firstly, if you have blown the whistle and signalled a penalty then you must stand by that and not award the goal. Ideally, you should have delayed your decision when the incident happened and you could then have allowed the goal by playing the advantage. You should also send off the goalkeeper.

EMBARRASSING MOMENT You have scored the winner, as embarrassing as that may be. You need to calm everyone down and explain that the officials are part of the field of play as are the bar, goalposts and corner flags. The goal must stand!

RUGBY TACKLE Award the goal and then show a yellow card to the defender for unsporting behaviour. You cannot give him a red card as the other attacker obviously had a goal-scoring opportunity so, in effect, the defender didn't deny that goal-scoring opportunity. You correctly played the advantage and the goal was scored.

PENALTY SHOOTOUT No, you do not. Only the players that finished the match may take penalties but what you do have to do is make the numbers even by instructing the other team to remove one of their penalty takers. If the player in question had come back onto the pitch before the final whistle at the end of extra time, he could have taken a penalty.

DID YOU KNOW?
HARRY COCHRANE

BORN: 24TH APRIL 2001

PLACE OF BIRTH: LAW, SOUTH LANARKSHIRE

He was among the first intake of the Scottish Football Association's Performance School programme, combining studies with football at Grange Academy in Kilmarnock.

Harry joined Hearts at U13 level and would go on to make his senior debut at the age of 16 during the 2017/18 campaign.

Harry wore the number 47 jersey in his first year of senior football but has since switched to number 20 for the 2018/19 season.

Harry's first goal for Hearts came in a pre-season friendly in Belfast prior to the 2017/18 campaign. He scored the opening goal in Hearts' 4-1 win against Linfield.

His competitive Hearts debut came against Dundee at Dens Park.

Harry's first goal for the Hearts was one to remember. Aged just 16, he opened the scoring in the Jambos' incredible 4-0 win against Celtic at Tynecastle in December 2017.

In April 2018, Harry committed his future to Hearts by signing a new deal that will keep him at Tynecastle until 2021.

ZDENĚK ZLÁMAL

Position: Goalkeeper

Nationality: Czech Republic

Date of Birth: 05/11/85

COLIN DOYLE

Position: Goalkeeper

Nationality: Rep. of Ireland

Date of Birth: 12/06/85

MICHAEL SMITH

Position: Defender

Nationality: Northern Ireland

Date of Birth: 04/09/88

JOHN SOUTTAR

Position: Defender

Nationality: Scotland

Date of Birth: 25/09/96

PETER HARING

Position: Defender

Nationality: Austria

Date of Birth: 02/06/93

CHRISTOPHE BERRA

Position: Defender

Nationality: Scotland

Date of Birth: 31/01/85

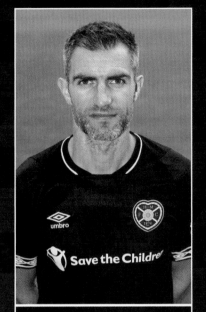

AARON HUGHES

Position: Defender

Nationality: Northern Ireland

Date of Birth: 08/11/79

BEN GARUCCIO

Position: Defender

Nationality: Australia

Date of Birth: 15/06/95

MARCUS GODINHO

Position: Defender

Nationality: Canada

Date of Birth: 28/06/97

JAMIE BRANDON

Position: Defender

Nationality: Scotland

Date of Birth: 05/02/98

Callumn Morrison

Position: Defender

Nationality: Scotland

Date of Birth: 05/07/99

OLLY LEE

Position: Midfielder

Nationality: England

Date of Birth: 11/07/91

ARNAUD DJOUM

Position: Midfielder

Nationality: Cameroon

Date of Birth: 02/05/89

OLIVER BOZANIC

Position: Midfielder

Nationality: Australia

Date of Birth: 08/01/89

HARRY COCHRANE

Position: Midfielder

Nationality: Scotland

Date of Birth: 24/04/01

RYAN EDWARDS

Position: Midfielder

Nationality: Australia

Date of Birth: 17/11/93

JAKE MULRANEY

Position: Midfielder

Nationality: Rep. of Ireland

Date of Birth: 05/04/96

ROSS CALLACHAN

Position: Midfielder

Nationality: Scotland

Date of Birth: 04/09/93

ANTHONY MCDONALD

Position: Midfielder

Nationality: Scotland

Date of Birth: 17/03/01

BOBBY BURNS

Position: Midfielder

Nationality: Northern Ireland

Date of Birth: 07/10/99

DANNY AMANKWAA

Position: Midfielder

Nationality: Denmark

Date of Birth: 30/01/94

LEWIS MOORE

Position: Midfielder

Nationality: Scotland

Date of Birth: 04/06/98

STEVEN MACLEAN

Position: Striker

Nationality: Scotland

Date of Birth: 23/08/82

UCHE IKPEAZU

Position: Striker

Nationality: England

Date of Birth: 28/02/95

STEVEN NAISMITH

Position: Striker

Nationality: Scotland

Date of Birth: 14/09/86

THAT TIME WE PLAYED...
HEARTS 4-0 MANCHESTER UNITED
JUNE 1ST 1960, LOS ANGELES

At the end of Hearts' title winning 1959/60 campaign, the team journeyed across the Atlantic for an extensive post-season tour of Canada and the US.

Between May 14th and June 9th, a total of ten games were played in Toronto, Ottawa, Montreal, Vancouver, Edmonton, New York City and Los Angeles. In addition to playing local teams, the Jambos also faced Manchester United on four separate occasions during the tour.

On May 14th they played out a 2-2 draw in Toronto, followed by a 3-0 United victory in New York eight days later. The Red Devils then ran out 3-2 winners in Vancouver on May 28th before the two sides met for a final time on June 1st. Los Angeles' Wrigley Field was the venue and the boys in maroon put in an impressive performance as they saw off United

June 1—Hearts 4 (Bauld (2), Crawford, Thomson (pen.); Manchester United 0—at Los Angeles.

Team—Marshall; Ferguson and Lough; Thomson, Milne, and Bowman; Smith, Murray, Bauld, Blackwood, and Crawford.

KING OF HEARTS

Tells his own Story of his 16 years at Tynecastle

2/-

five hour time difference, they were able to watch the European Cup Final, this year staged back home in Scotland at Glasgow's Hampden Park.

"The Hearts squad were captivated by the likes of Ferenc Puskás, Alfredo Di Stéfano, Francisco Gento, Argentinean José Santamaría and Captain José María Zárraga as Real Madrid and Eintracht Frankfurt entertained majestically."

He also touches on Hearts and United's time spent in LA:

"Both clubs travelled together, chartering a plane to take them to Los Angeles after refueling in Seattle and San Francisco. At one refueling, out came the dreaded tartan song-books once more, and the Hearts players were even benevolent enough to share their book with their Manchester United foes, as both sets of players and staff belted out Shirley Bassey's "Kiss Me, Honey, Honey"!

"The two teams were again staying in the same hotel, in the city's Hollywood district.

"The players from both clubs socialised together during their three days off, going to Long Beach, Santa Monica and visiting the set of MGM Pictures. They went to a baseball game, cheering for the LA Dodgers, and Gordon found there was great camaraderie amongst the players of both Hearts and Manchester United when off the field."

by four goals to nil. Goals came courtesy of George Thomson, Ian Crawford and a Willie Bauld brace.

The game was played before a crowd of 10,500 at Wrigley Field, a stadium more accustomed to baseball than soccer. That being said, it did host a friendly between the US and England a year earlier, in which the English defeated the hosts 8-1.

Wrigley Field was home to Minor League Baseball side Los Angeles Angels, who in fact joined Major League Baseball four months after Hearts' visit. In 1962, the Angels moved to the Dodger Stadium, leaving Wrigley Field empty for most of the year. It staged a Martin Luther King rally in 1963 as well as the odd American Football match and boxing events; however, it was nonetheless deemed surplus to requirements and demolished in 1969.

One of the Hearts players in action in LA was ex-Hibs striker Gordon Smith. In his book, "Prince of Wingers", he fondly remembers the overseas tour and tells the tale of how Hearts and Matt Busby's Manchester United travelled together, with the players exploring the various cities during their time off.

Recalling the night they all gathered in Montreal to watch the European Cup final on TV, Smith notes:

"The players were glued to the hotel lobby television on the afternoon of 18th May. Due to the

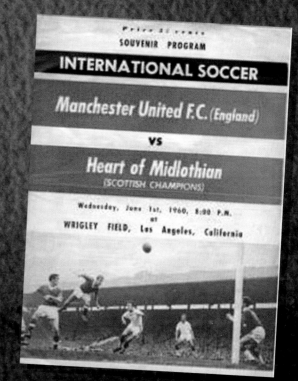

SOUVENIR PROGRAM

INTERNATIONAL SOCCER

Manchester United F.C. (England)

vs

Heart of Midlothian (SCOTTISH CHAMPIONS)

Wednesday, June 1st, 1960, 8:00 P.M. at WRIGLEY FIELD, Los Angeles, California

THAT TIME WE PLAYED...
HEARTS 4-2 MACCABI TEL AVIV
AUGUST 1ST 1966, TYNECASTLE

The Israeli Cup holders arrived in Edinburgh for a clash with the Jambos in August '66 as part of their extensive tour of the UK and Europe.

Hearts had spent the week leading up to this friendly at a training camp in Dunkeld and although they saw this fixture as an important part of their pre-season, their main focus was very much on a League Cup showdown with Celtic 12 days later.

Celtic manager Jock Stein was among the 5,000 strong crowd that turned out for this Monday night encounter in Gorgie. It took just three minutes for the hosts to get their noses in front as Willie Wallace guided a cross from the right into the net.

The Israelis drew level seven minutes later, however, thanks to a mistake from Hearts' 20 year old debutant goalkeeper, Jim McGinley. Maccabi's Asis hit a speculative shot that rolled through McGinley's legs, much to the dismay of the Hearts 'keeper.

His horror was short lived, however, as the Jambos restored their lead inside 60 seconds. Davie Holt bombed down the right flank and hit a pin-point cross into the box for Wallace to head home. The Hearts number 9 then sealed his hat-trick in the second half when he fired home a rebound on 62 minutes. The Maroons' fourth goal came two minutes later when George Miller lashed home a low shot.

WILLIE WALLACE, of Hearts, was Scotland's centre as they fought for a place in the last sixteen.

The visitors pulled a goal back through Schipgel on 80 minutes, however, the game ended in a Hearts victory.

Despite finding the net on four occasions, the next day's newspaper reports were less than complimentary about Hearts performance. One bemoaned the lack of cutting edge in the match and singled out Wallace as the only flash point:

"Wallace must have been one of the few players on the field who could have had reason to feel satisfaction with his display in the first game of the season.

"Hearts adopted the 4-2-4 formation of last season and the defence looked very solid, although the Israeli side did not provide a very tough work-out."

Another report noted that "Maccabi's slow-motion tactics, plus the lush Tynecastle turf, killed any hopes of this being a fast game." It added that "indecision, especially in midfield, bogged the game down with the ball being slowly and tantalisingly switched across the field."

It is hard to judge just how much the watching Celtic manager learned from Hearts' performance, however, it appeared to be enough for him to mastermind a victory in Gorgie 12 days later. On August 13th, Celtic ran out 2-0 winners thanks to a John McBride double.

Hearts had experimented by making the match an all-ticket game; however, it didn't quite go to plan if one newspaper report is to be believed:

"The controversial Hearts plan for a 48,000 all-ticket opener with Celtic at increased prices ended in a shambles at Tynecastle yesterday.

"There were 23,000 fans missing, including 5,000 ticket-holders! The official attendance was given as just over 25,000.

"Hearts are now likely to scrap all-ticket matches – unless the police advise it – and will think very seriously before upping admission charges again."

The hat-trick hero from the Maccabi game, Willie Wallace, played against Celtic that day. Although he didn't get on the scoresheet, he had clearly made an impression of Jock Stein, who moved to sign him later that year. In December 1966, Jock got his man for an estimated £30,000 – the most Celtic had ever paid for a player, according to Jock himself.

THAT TIME WE PLAYED...
VÅLERENGA 1-3 HEARTS
OCTOBER 27TH 1965, OSLO

The Inter-Cities Fairs Cup Fairs Cup was established in 1955 with a view to promote international trade fairs. Rather than having teams qualify based on their domestic league positions, the tournament was instead open to any teams based in cities that hosted trade fairs. The Cup ran for a total of 16 years before falling under the control of UEFA, who quickly re-branded it as the UEFA Cup (today's Europa League) in 1971.

In 1965, Hearts were entered into the early rounds of the competition and found themselves paired with Norwegian side Vålerenga. The Oslo based club were a somewhat familiar opposition as the two teams had met just four months prior during the Jambos' pre-season tour of Norway. Hearts won 4-1 that day and were expecting a similar result when Vålerenga arrived in Gorgie on October 18th for the first leg.

A crowd of roughly 9,000 turned out at Tynecastle on a Monday evening for a 7.30pm kick-off. A Willie Wallace goal on the stroke of half-time earned Tommy Walker's men a 1-0 victory on the night. A positive result, but one that should have been far more comfortable if the next day's match report is to be believed:

"Hearts Fairs Cup hopes were dimmed by unbelievably bad finishing," began Davie Laing's verdict.

"Their attempts to put the ball into the net were as woeful as anything they have served up this season. The Norwegian officials and players were cock-a-hoop with the result – and were confidently predicting victory for Vålerenga next week," it continued.

The Jambos' relatively poor showing could perhaps be attributed to the fact they had played out a 3-3 draw with Partick Thistle just two days prior. Nevertheless, the boys in maroon journeyed to Norway the following week fully determined to put the tie to bed.

The return leg took place at Oslo's Bislett Stadium, a ground more commonly associated with athletics. During the winter months it was also used to host speed skating events. Bislett served as Vålerenga's home until 1999 and has been fully redeveloped in recent years as it continues to serve as a prominent athletics venue.

On Wednesday 27th October 1965, a crowd of 15,000 turned out to watch Hearts beat the hosts 3-1. Any concerns the Jambos may have had about a Vålerenga comeback were put to bed early doors when Don Kerrigan fired in the opener on nine minutes. Tommy Traynor added a second on 22 minutes to put the Gorgie boys 3-0 up on aggregate.

A Per Knudsen consolation goal temporarily sparked the match back into life on 71 minutes; however, Kerrigan added a third just before the final whistle to secure a comfortable 3-1 win for the Edinburgh side. The match report noted it had been a largely one-sided affair, although Vålerenga's strike did offer the hosts some hope late on:

"Vålerenga responded to cheering from their fans by putting up a fight, but as they were still two behind on aggregate it was impossible for the small Scottish contingent in the stand to share the belated enthusiasm of a crowd which had been whistling and jeering the Oslo players earlier."

The report continued: "Once a faint possibility of trouble ahead was emphasised by Knudsen's goal, the Tynecastle men rolled up their shiny white sleeves and sailed with great momentum into opponents who really should not have been allowed to raise their supporters' hopes in the first place."

The article also makes reference to Hearts' white kit, which was indeed loaned to them by their opponents in order to avoid a clash. Also noted was the pre-match entertainment, which saw a Norwegian band play a rousing rendition of 'Scotland the Brave'.

The Jambos returned to their homeland with a comfortable 4-1 aggregate win in the bag and would go on to face Spanish opposition in the next round. Following a 3-3 draw at home to Real Zaragoza they played out a 2-2 draw away. The third and final tie ended in a 1-0 loss to a side that would go on to lose the final to FC Barcelona.

With regards to Vålerenga, it is worth noting a couple of prominent names who featured against Hearts. The first is Nils Arne Eggen, a 24 year old defender at the time. After his playing career he entered management and enjoyed several spells in charge of Rosenborg BK. The most significant reign took place between 1988 and 2002, when he led the Trondheim side to 11 consecutive league titles. During that time they played in the Champions League for eight straight seasons, famously defeating the likes of AC Milan, Borussia Dortmund and Real Madrid. Eggen's dedication to an attacking, 4-3-3 formation football earned his team plaudits around Europe and he remains one of the most influential Norwegian managers of all-time.

The same can certainly be said for another member of the Vålerenga team that faced Hearts. At the time, Egil 'Drillo' Olsen was a tricky winger who earned his 'Drillo' nickname thanks to his habit of dribbling opponents. It was in management, however, where he gained international recognition. As Norway's national team boss, he took his country to the 1994 and 1998 World Cups, famously beating Brazil in the group stages of France '98.

A pragmatic manager, he was often referred to as 'The Professor' due to his seemingly insatiable appetite for statistical information. A pioneer within video analysis, he left no stone unturned in a bid to work out the best way of breaking down opponents. Recognising Norway's lack of technical ability, he set about forming a 4-5-1 formation with a heavy focus on counter attacks. Long balls forward to tall wingers was the name of the game, which often attracted criticism from opposing fans, players and managers alike. His success with Norway at the time cannot be discounted, however, and he later went on to manage Vålerenga, Wimbledon and Iraq before returning for a second spell in charge of Norway in 1999.

DID YOU KNOW?
OLLY LEE

BORN: 11TH JULY 1991
PLACE OF BIRTH: LONDON

Lee was on the books at West Ham as a youngster.

He is the son of ex-England international Robert Lee, who was also a midfielder.

Robert Lee was a key figure in Kevin Keegan's Newcastle United side during the 1990s.

Whilst at West Ham, Olly went out on loan to Dagenham & Redbridge and Gillingham.

He later moved to Barnet and then Birmingham City before signing for Luton Town in 2015.

Whilst at Luton, Olly played alongside his younger brother,

Elliot. The pair helped their team win promotion in 2017/18.

Olly scored 11 goals in 124 games for Luton Town. He also had 17 assists to his name.

Olly grew up supporting Newcastle United, the team his Dad played for.

PLAYER OF THE YEAR AWARDS 2017/18

PLAYERS, STAFF AND SUPPORTERS GATHERED AT TYNECASTLE ON SUNDAY 8TH APRIL 2018 FOR THE CLUB'S ANNUAL PLAYER OF THE YEAR AWARDS, SPONSORED BY MERCEDES-BENZ OF EDINBURGH.

The Hearts Youth Development Committee received the Special Recognition Award to thank them for 27 years of incredible support.

Craig Levein picked up the George Nicolson Award in recognition of the role he has played in helping to develop the Hearts Academy, whilst Club Photographer Ron MacNeill received the Doc Melvin Award for his years of dedication to Heart of Midlothian Football Club.

The Celebration of Youth Awards saw Sean Ward crowned the U17s POTY. Chris Hamilton picked up the award for the U20s POTY before John Souttar was named the Overall Young Player of the Year.

The first of the fans' awards went to Demetri Mitchell for his goal of the season against St Johnstone. The 4-0 victory over Celtic in December 2017 was voted the most memorable moment of the season, much to the delight of the sell-out crowd in the Gorgie Suite.

Finally, captain Christophe Berra was a double winner on the night as he picked up both the Fan's Player of the Year and the Players' Player of the Year.

GEORGE NICOLSON AWARD WINNER CRAIG LEVEIN

HEART OF MIDLOTHIAN FOOTBALL CLUB

PLAYER OF THE YEAR 2017-2018

Sponsored by Mercedes-Benz of

**DOC MELVIN AWARD
WINNER RON MACNEILL**

U17S POTY SEAN WARD

U20 POTY CHRIS HAMILTON

OVERALL YPOTY IS JOHN SOUTTAR

GOAL OF THE SEASON WENT TO DEMETRI MITCHELL

HARRY COCHRANE COLLECTED THE MEMORABLE MOMENT AWARD

DOUBLE AWARD WINNER CHRISTOPHE BERRA

HE BIG TYNIE QUIZ

YOUR HEARTS KNOWLEDGE TO THE TEST!

Heart of Midlothian Football Club was founded in which year?

When did Hearts last win the Scottish Cup?

What's the name of Hearts' beloved mascot?

What position did manager Craig Levein play during his playing days?

What country does Aaron Hughes play for?

6. What squad number does Olly Lee wear?

7. True or False: Steven Naismith has never played in the English Premier League?

8. Which Hearts player has won the Africa Cup of Nations?

9. How old was Harry Cochrane when he scored his first senior goal against Celtic in December 2017?

Save the Children

10. What nationality is Ben Garuccio?

11. How many goals did Kyle Lafferty score for Hearts in the 2017/18 season?

12. True or False: Harry Kane made his Tottenham Hotspur debut against Hearts?

13. Hearts legend John Robertson's nickname was what? The Hammer of the Hibs or The Hammer of Gorgie?

14. How many goals did Rudi Skacel score in the 2012 Scottish Cup final against Hibs?

15. Which city did Christophe Berra grow up in?

16. Which club did Hearts sign John Souttar from?

17. True or False: Steven MacLean has never won the Scottish Cup?

18. Which Hearts legend had the nickname 'The King of Hearts'?

19. Who is the Hearts Reserves coach?

20. Where is the Hearts training centre?

CELEBRATING THE HEROES OF '98!

ALMOST EVERY MEMBER OF HEARTS' 1998 SCOTTISH CUP WINNING SQUAD WAS IN ATTENDANCE AT THE '98 CELEBRATION DINNER AT THE EDINBURGH INTERNATIONAL CONFERENCE CENTRE ON MAY 20TH 2018.

The heroes of '98 were joined by over 800 Jambos for an evening that will live long in the memory. The 20th anniversary celebrations kicked off with every squad member being welcomed on to the stage to rapturous applause.

Willie Young, the match referee in the '98 final, then sounded his whistle to signal the start of a minute's applause for the late Stefano Salvatori. Willie later returned to the stage for a fantastic performance as Guest Speaker.

AN EMOTIONAL ROUND OF APPLAUSE FOR SALVATORI

THE CLASS OF '98

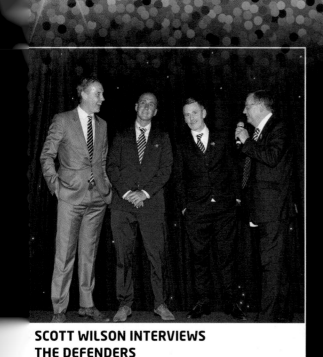

SCOTT WILSON INTERVIEWS THE DEFENDERS

On a highly emotional night, Stefano's wife Gillian made a wonderful speech to the sell-out crowd, prompting a rousing chorus of 'Salvatori, Salvatori, Ole, Ole, Ole' to ring out from every corner of the room.

A total of four awards were handed out on the evening to some very deserving recipients. The Special Award, sponsored by The Football Company, went to Hearts' legendary goalkeeper, Gordon Marshall Snr. He was a key component of the 1957/58 side and picked up an award that recognised both his own and his team's marvellous achievements.

Stéphane Adam then picked up the Goal of the Tournament Award, sponsored by Charles

PLAYER OF THE TOURNAMENT NEIL MCCANN

Henshaw & Sons Ltd, for his strike against Rangers in the final. Gilles Rousset's save to deny Lorenzo Amoruso was voted the Save of the Tournament.

Finally, Neil McCann received the Player of the Tournament Award, sponsored by St Andrews Timber & Building Supplies Ltd. All three of the tournament awards were voted for by the fans.

Special thanks go to Headline Sponsor, ASC Scaffolding, and to Paterson's Trophy Supplies for providing the award trophies.

Last but not least, Scott "The Voice of Hearts" Wilson was once again in a league of his own as the host for the evening.

THE BACKROOM STAFF

GORDON MARSHALL COLLECTS HIS AWARD

53

DID YOU KNOW?

UCHE IKPEAZU

BORN: 28TH FEBUARY 1995
PLACE OF BIRTH: BEDFORD

Uche grew up in the north London borough of Wembley.

As a youngster he played boys' club football with Manchester City and England star Raheem Sterling.

In 2012/13, he scored 28 goals for Reading's academy team – making him the highest scorer at academy level in England that season.

Uche joined Hearts from Cambridge United in the summer of 2018.

He scored during his Tynecastle debut against Cowdenbeath in the Betfred Cup and followed it up with a brace against Inverness CT a few days later.

Uche was born on February 28, 1995. He stands 6ft 3 inches tall.

RYAN EDWARDS

So...what is your hometown and where exactly is it?
I'm from Perth in Australia, which is a city on the western side of the country.

How would you describe it someone who has never set foot there?
It's a bit underestimated, I think. Most people who travel Down Under head to Sydney or Melbourne, but Perth's actually one of the most beautiful cities in the country. It's got great beaches, brilliant weather and a really nice, laid-back vibe.

Most famous person to hail from Perth?
Aside from you, obviously...
The first person that comes to mind is Sam Worthington, the actor who had a lead role in the Avatar movie. He's from a town that's around half an hour's drive from Perth, so I think that counts?

What's your favourite part of the city?
I grew up roughly ten minutes away from this great strip called Fremantle. I went to school there and spent a lot of time hanging out there. It's close to the beach so you get some amazing sunsets and it also has good nightlife. There's some top spots for coffee and ice cream as well, so it's well worth a visit.

Favourite restaurant?
Tough one. My favourite one is in a weird location as it sits just off one of the main highways, it's called Welcome Noodle House. They serve the best BBQ pork I've ever tasted and I've struggled to find BBQ pork of a similar standard here in the UK!

If someone had one day to spend in Perth, what should they get up to?
Head to Fremantle or the city centre. You also can't go there without checking out the beaches. I'd recommend Scarborough or City Beach. Then you've got Cottesloe which has beautiful scenery and some good beach clubs for drinks.

How often do you go back home?
I've not been back for a couple of years now. I usually go back in the close season for a couple of weeks but I haven't in a while. I've had my family over for Christmas for the past few years so that's the most important thing for me. The problem is that when I go back in close season then it's in the middle of winter over there. So you're looking at 15 degrees tops, so I'd rather just go on holiday in Europe to be honest!

BOBBY BURNS

So where exactly is your hometown?

I'm from a village called Crumlin in Northern Ireland. It's about a half hour drive from Belfast in County Antrim.

How would you describe Crumlin to someone who has never been there before?

Ehm... it's small and there's not much to do. There's only a few thousand people living there so it's a got a good community feel to it. The people are all really nice and there's a decent park and a few good walks to be had.

Any famous residents?

Stephen Robinson, the Motherwell manager, is from Crumlin. But that's about it to be honest, I can't think of anyone else.

Where did you hang out as a kid?

That would probably be the main park, I played a lot of football there as a boy. The park is actually called Burns Park. I'd always pretend it was named after me but it's actually named after my grandfather. He was a local councillor who did a lot of work within the community so they named it after him when he passed away. It's got a lot of good facilities with a few five and seven-a-side cages that I've spent a lot of time playing in over the years.

Favourite place to eat?

Apart from at home, you mean? There's a nice ice cream café in town, it's pretty decent so I would probably say that.

If someone had a whole day to spend in Crumlin, what should they do?

Leave as quickly as possible!

No, I'm only joking. I would probably recommend some of the walking routes, they're really nice. There's a glen and a decent forest walk so I would go for that. We also have a good Gaelic football team so you could maybe head along and watch them?

P38-39: WHERE'S JOCK?

P21: WORDSEARCH

G	C	T	L	R	D	J	R	B	F
B	H	O	A	R	R	E	B	B	N
N	N	L	C	D	V	C	K	S	I
E	A	E	L	H	K	Q	O	G	K
I	E	V	L	A	R	B	N	D	P
G	L	E	R	N	M	A	R	V	E
R	C	I	W	A	L	A	N	B	A
O	A	N	J	E	R	P	L	E	Z
G	M	M	E	G	X	L	K	Z	U
S	O	U	T	T	A	R	J	M	F

P48: BIG TYNIE QUIZ

1. 1874
2. 2012
3. Jock the Jambo
4. Defender
5. Northern Ireland
6. 8
7. False
8. Arnaud Djoum
9. 16 years old
10. Australian
11. 19
12. True
13. Hibs
14. 2
15. Edinburgh
16. Dundee United
17. False
18. Willie Bauld
19. Andy Kirk
20. Riccarton